The Jerusalem Council

By Michael Penny

ISBN 978 1 78364 635 7

THE OPEN BIBLE TRUST
Fordland Mount, Upper Basildon,
Reading, RG8 8LU, UK.

www.obt.org.uk

The Jerusalem Council

Contents

Introduction

To fully appreciate the reason for the Jerusalem Council and its decision, we first need to give some background. We will start with the first Missionary Journey of Paul and Barnabas (Acts chapters 13 and 14).

They left Antioch in Syria, accompanied by John Mark, and set sail for Cyprus, which was familiar territory as Barnabas was from that island (Acts 4:36). They arrived in Salamis, on the east shore, and spoke at the synagogue there and no doubt at many other synagogues as they travelled through the whole island. Nothing untoward is recorded in Acts and it would appear they had a trouble-free time.

Eventually they came to Paphos, on the west. There they spoke to the Roman proconsul but were opposed by a Jewish sorcerer whom Paul struck blind. The result of this miracle of judgment[1] was that the proconsul believed in the Lord.

But where to now? Sail back to Caesarea and report to the elders in Jerusalem? No! They decided to sail north to Perga in Pamphylia, with the aim of going into the Province of Galatia to take in the cities of Antioch, Iconium, Lystra and Derbe. However, the thought of going there caused John Mark to desert them (Acts 13:13; 15:38). What caused this reaction in John Mark?

---

[1] For more on the miracles of judgment which took place during the Acts Period see pages 137-146 of *The Miracles of the Apostles* by Michael Penny, published by The Open Bible Trust.

1. The Jews of the Dispersion

At the Pentecost of Acts 2 we read that there were God-fearing Jews from every nation under heaven. However, when we read universal words like 'every' we need to be careful. We use such words in our language all the time, but seldom do we give them a literal, universal meaning; e.g. is everyone here?

Acts 2 lists those cities and states where the Jews came from. We read of Jews from many places including Cappadocia (to the east of Galatia), from Pontus (to the north), from Phrygia and Asia (to the west), and from Pamphylia (to the south). However, we do not read of any Jews from Galatia and there is no mention of Pisidian Antioch, Iconium, Lystra and Derbe. Many of the Jews from these places were Hellenized. They still attended synagogues but many had adopted Greek practices, married Greeks and had strayed from the Law of Moses (e.g. Timothy had not been circumcised: Acts 16:1-3). What sort of reaction would a Pharisee like Paul and a Levite like Barnabas receive? And how would these *laissez faire* Jews react to the teaching that a carpenter, one Jesus of Nazareth, was the Messiah? John Mark may have feared for his safety, and he was right.

2. Success, Opposition and Persecution

Paul and Barnabas continued alone and in Pisidian Antioch they spoke in the synagogue to an audience of Jews and Proselytes[2], and to some God-fearing Gentiles who also were in attendance.

In Pisidian Antioch

Success

> As Paul and Barnabas were leaving the synagogue, the people invited them to speak further about these things on the next Sabbath. When the congregation was dismissed, many of the Jews and devout converts to Judaism followed Paul and Barnabas, who talked with them and urged them to continue in the grace of God. On the next Sabbath almost the whole city gathered to hear the word of the Lord. (Acts 13:42-44)

Opposition

> When the Jews [i.e. the 'leadership' verse 50] saw the crowds, they were filled with jealousy. They began to contradict what Paul was saying and heaped abuse on him. (Acts 13:45)

Success

---

[2] Proselytes is the term used of those Gentiles who converted to Judaism. To do so they had to keep the covenant of circumcision and the Sabbath; e.g. see Isaiah 56:6-8.

Then Paul and Barnabas answered them boldly ... "We now turn to the Gentiles. For this is what the Lord has commanded us: 'I have made you a light for the Gentiles, that you may bring salvation to the end of the earth.'" When the Gentiles heard this, they were glad and honoured the word of the Lord; and all who were appointed for eternal life believed. The word of the Lord spread through the whole region. (Acts 13:46-49)

Persecution

But the Jewish leaders incited the God-fearing women of high standing and the leading men of the city [i.e. the Gentile leaders]. They stirred up persecution against Paul and Barnabas, and expelled them from their region. (Acts 13:50)

On to Iconium

Success

At Iconium Paul and Barnabas went as usual into the Jewish synagogue. There they spoke so effectively that a great number of Jews and Greeks believed. (Acts 14:1)

Opposition

But the Jews who refused to believe stirred up the other Gentiles and poisoned their minds against the brothers. (Acts 14:2)

Success

So Paul and Barnabas spent considerable time there, speaking boldly for the Lord, who confirmed the message of his grace by enabling them to perform signs and wonders. (Acts 14:3)

The people of the city were divided; some sided with the Jews, others with the apostles. There was a plot afoot among both Gentiles and Jews, together with their leaders, to mistreat them and stone them. (Acts 14:4-5)

In Lystra

Success

In Lystra there sat a man who was lame. He had been that way from birth and had never walked. He listened to Paul as he was speaking. Paul looked directly at him, saw that he had faith to be healed [saved[3]] and called out, "Stand up on your feet!" At that, the man jumped up and began to walk. (Acts 14:8-10)

Opposition and Persecution

Then some Jews came from Antioch and Iconium and won the crowd over. They stoned Paul and dragged him outside the city, thinking he was dead. (Acts 14:19)

---

[3] The word translated 'healed' in the Greek is *sozo* whose main meaning is 'saved' and is translated 'save' in 92 of its 108 occurrences. For a thorough treatment of this word, and the usual Greek word for healing (*therapeuo* and *iaomai*) see *The Miracles of the Apostles* by Michael Penny, pages 109-113, published by The Open Bible Trust.

3. The return journey

From Lystra they went on to Derbe where they preached the good news and won a large number of disciples (Acts 14:21). Then, amazingly, Paul and Barnabas decided to retrace their steps and return to those cities where they had been so badly treated! Their reason for doing so was to strengthen the disciples and appoint elders in each church and to encourage the new converts to remain true to the faith. He also told them that "We must go through many hardships" (Acts 14:21-23).

From there they journeyed south and sailed back to Antioch in Syria, and we read that they stayed there a long time (Acts 14:28). Undoubtedly, they needed rest and recuperation from such a tiring and trying trip … but their peace and tranquillity was broken.

4. News from Galatia

While Paul was in Syrian Antioch news reached him from Galatia, but it was not good news. There arose a group of Christian Jews who are often termed the Judaisers or the circumcision group. These were Christian Jews who believed that Jesus was the Christ (Messiah), the Son of God and the Saviour but they did not fully understand the gospel of salvation by grace through faith in Christ. They knew that faith in Christ was *necessary* for salvation, but they did not understand that it was *sufficient*. They taught that the Gentiles also had to be circumcised. Considering all the opposition Paul had overcome in Galatia and the persecution he had endured, I am sure Paul would have liked to have gone back to Galatia immediately, but he could not. Instead he wrote, stating that:

> I am astonished that you are so quickly deserting the one who called you to live in the grace of Christ and are turning to a different gospel— which is really no gospel at all. Evidently some people are throwing you into confusion and are trying to pervert the gospel of Christ. (Galatians 1:6-7)

For Paul this gospel of 'faith' plus 'circumcision' was a perversion of the true gospel and was not really 'good news'. However, if this was so important to Paul, why didn't he journey back to Galatia immediately? It would appear he had the same problem in Antioch, only worse!

5. Problems with Peter

It seems Peter journeyed to Antioch in Syria, to see what was going on there as this was the first city where the Gospel had been openly preached to the Gentiles (Acts 11:19-21). Also, he may well have wanted to see Paul and Barnabas and hear how they had fared on Cyprus and elsewhere. After all, he had been part of the group which agreed that Paul and Barnabas should go to the Gentile nations (Galatians 2:9). However, while there, some Judaisers (the circumcision group) came down from Jerusalem.

> When Cephas [Peter] came to Antioch, I opposed him to his face, because he stood condemned. For before certain men came from James[4], he used to eat with the Gentiles. But when they arrived, he began to draw back and separate himself from the Gentiles because he was afraid of those who belonged to the circumcision group. The other Jews joined him in his hypocrisy, so that by their hypocrisy even Barnabas was led astray. (Galatians 2:11-13)

It appears, for a while, that Paul stood almost alone, but we learn later that both Peter and Barnabas got back on track.

It seems at first these Judaisers just advocated separation from the Gentiles, especially at meal times. However, they were soon to go further.

> Certain people came down from Judea to Antioch and were teaching the believers: "Unless you are circumcised,

---

[4] Paul was later to learn that although this group 'said' they had come from James, they did not have his authority, nor that of the other Apostles in Jerusalem (see Acts 15:24).

according to the custom taught by Moses, you cannot be saved." (Acts 15:1)

However, by this time Barnabas was standing alongside Paul.

> This brought Paul and Barnabas into sharp dispute and debate with them. So Paul and Barnabas were appointed, along with some other believers, to go up to Jerusalem to see the apostles and elders about this question. (Acts 15:2)

An important point to note here is that Paul and Barnabas did not win the argument; they could not convince the leaders of the church in Antioch that their teaching was correct and that the Judaisers were wrong, that this circumcision group was perverting the gospel of salvation by grace through faith. Why did these Judaisers think circumcision was so important and necessary for salvation? And what arguments could they have put forward to support their case?

6. Circumcision

God had made a covenant of circumcision with Abraham, the terms of which were as follows:

> Then God said to Abraham, "As for you, you must keep my covenant, you and your descendants after you for the generations to come. This is my covenant with you and your descendants after you, the covenant you are to keep: Every male among you shall be circumcised. You are to undergo circumcision, and it will be the sign of the covenant between me and you. For the generations to come every male among you who is eight days old must be circumcised, including those born in your household or bought with money from a foreigner—those who are not your offspring. Whether born in your household or bought with your money, they must be circumcised. My covenant in your flesh is to be an everlasting covenant. Any uncircumcised male, who has not been circumcised in the flesh, will be cut off from his people; he has broken my covenant." (Genesis 17:9-14)

Here the instruction was not only for Abraham and his descendants (verse 9), but also for "every male among you", including those bought from a foreigner. Anyone not circumcised was to be cut off.

Following the Passover and the exodus from Egypt "many other people" [a mixed multitude, *KJV*] came out of Egypt with the people of Israel (Exodus 12:38). Concerning future celebrations of the Passover, we read that:

> The LORD said to Moses and Aaron, "These are the regulations for the Passover meal: "No foreigner may eat it. Any slave you have bought may eat it after you have

circumcised him, but a temporary resident or a hired worker may not eat it. It must be eaten inside the house; take none of the meat outside the house. Do not break any of the bones. The whole community of Israel must celebrate it. A foreigner residing among you who wants to celebrate the LORD's Passover must have all the males in his household circumcised; then he may take part like one born in the land. No uncircumcised male may eat it." (Exodus 12:43-48)

Here we see circumcision became necessary, not just for one bought from a foreigner (a slave), but also for any Gentile who wished to become part of Israel. And this is the teaching of the Law of Moses and is the theme throughout the Old Testament. For example, in Isaiah 56:4-7:

> For this is what the LORD says:
> "To the eunuchs who keep my Sabbaths,
>   who choose what pleases me
>   and hold fast to my covenant [of circumcision]—
> to them I will give within my temple and its walls
>   a memorial and a name
>   better than sons and daughters;
> I will give them an everlasting name
>   that will endure forever.
> And foreigners who bind themselves to the LORD
>   to minister to him,
> to love the name of the LORD,
>   and to be his servants,
> all who keep the Sabbath without desecrating it
>   and who hold fast to my covenant [of circumcision]—
> these I will bring to my holy mountain
>   and give them joy in my house of prayer.
> Their burnt offerings and sacrifices
>   will be accepted on my altar;

for my house will be called
a house of prayer for all nations."

Thus anyone in any condition and from any nation could become part of the people of Israel, but one necessary condition is that they had to be circumcised. Therefore, the Judaisers had much from their Scriptures (our Old Testament) that could support their case, but there was more.

7. Recent practice

The *Pax Romana* (Latin for "Roman Peace") was the long period of relative peace established by Caesar Augustus in about 27 BC. There was peace and safety, as well as freedom of religion, throughout the Empire. During this time a number of Gentiles, some of whom had become disillusioned with the practices and shallowness of the pagan temples, started to attend the synagogues of the dispersion and these are referred to in the Acts of the Apostles as God-fearers, or God-fearing Gentiles. These sat in a separate section of the synagogue and they could travel up to Jerusalem and enter the outer courts of the temple. However, should they wish to, they could undergo circumcision and join themselves to the people of Israel. They could then enter the inner courts of the Jerusalem temple. In the Acts these are referred to as Proselytes or converts to Judaism.

Another reason why there were so many God-fearing Gentiles and Proselytes in the synagogues of the dispersion during the period of time covered by the Acts of the Apostles was that the Jews (and especially the Jews of the Dispersion) had, for possibly the only time in their history, embarked on active proselytising. This would mean not only encouraging the Gentiles to attend the synagogues and become God-fearers, but also encouraging those God-fearers to go a step further and undergo circumcision. Thus for something like thirty or more years before Peter went to the God-fearing Gentile Cornelius, and before the Christian Jews started preaching to the Greeks in Syrian Antioch, the Jews had actively been practising circumcision amongst Gentile converts – in accordance with the Law of Moses and the Old Testament Scriptures.

All this being the case, we can, perhaps, have a better appreciation of just how strong a case the Judaisers put to the Jewish Christian leaders in Antioch. So much so that those leaders could not decide between their arguments and those of Paul and Barnabas. They decided to resolve their dilemma by sending both groups to Jerusalem for the Apostles and elders there to sort out the problem. But what arguments would Paul and Barnabas have put forward? We will discuss this more fully when we come to the Council meeting.

8. On to Jerusalem

From Syrian Antioch Paul and Barnabas travelled to Phoenicia and Samaria, reporting to the believers there how Gentiles in Galatia and elsewhere had been converted. When they arrived in Jerusalem the church and the Apostles welcomed them and they reported everything God had done through them but …

> Then some of the believers who belonged to the party of the Pharisees stood up and said, "The Gentiles must be circumcised and required to keep the Law of Moses." (Acts 15:5)

Thus this problem was everywhere: not only in Galatia and Syria, but even in Jerusalem. Before moving on, we need to make two comments about this verse.

1) Note first that these people are referred to as 'believers'; i.e. they were Christians. They did not fully understand the gospel of salvation by grace through faith, but if people believe that Christ died for their sins and rose again from the dead … they are saved; they are Christians … even if they think they have to do something else (e.g. be circumcised; be baptised; make confessions). A person is saved by faith in Christ, not by faith in the gospel or in understanding the gospel.

2) Second: we should not read into this verse that these believing Pharisees were saying that the Gentiles had to keep the Law of Moses to be saved. We know from elsewhere that the Judaisers did say they had to be circumcised to be saved, but the keeping of the Law was something Gentiles should do after they were saved – according this group of Pharisaic Judaisers.

So the apostles and elders met in Jerusalem to discuss these issues: did the Gentiles need to be circumcised to be saved, and, after being saved, did they need to obey the Law of Moses?

9. The Jerusalem Council

We are told in Acts 15:7 that there was "much discussion". We are given no information as to the arguments put forward by the Judaisers, but I have suggested above two lines of argument they may have put forward.

Also we have just a brief synopsis of what Peter said, and have but half a sentence relating to Paul and Barnabas. After that James gives the verdict.

11. Peter's address

After much discussion, Peter got up and addressed them: "Brothers, you know that some time ago God made a choice among you that the Gentiles might hear from my lips the message of the gospel and believe. God, who knows the heart, showed that he accepted them by giving the Holy Spirit to them, just as he did to us. He did not discriminate between us and them, for he purified their hearts by faith. Now then, why do you try to test God by putting on the necks of Gentiles a yoke that neither we nor our ancestors have been able to bear? No! We believe it is through the grace of our Lord Jesus that we are saved, just as they are." (Acts 15:7-11)

Some people like to point out Peter's failures but if we look carefully at the life of Peter, he often bounces back and puts right what he has said or done wrong. He had caused great problems in Syrian Antioch a little earlier, as we read about above (Galatians 2:11-13). However, strong words from Paul seem to have brought both Peter and Barnabas to their senses.

When I saw that they [Peter and Barnabas] were not acting in line with the truth of the gospel, I said to Cephas [Peter] in front of them all, "You are a Jew, yet you live like a Gentile and not like a Jew. How is it, then, that you force Gentiles to follow Jewish customs? We who are Jews by birth and not sinful Gentiles know that a person is not justified by the works of the law, but by faith in Jesus Christ. So we, too, have put our faith in Christ Jesus that we may be justified by faith in Christ and not by the works of the law, because by the works of the law no one will be justified … I have been crucified with Christ and I no longer live, but Christ lives in me. The life I now live in the body, I live by faith in the Son of God, who loved me and gave himself for me. I do not set aside the grace of God, for if righteousness could be gained through the law, Christ died for nothing!" (Galatians 2:14-16; 20-21)

Paul emphatically emphasised to these two brothers that as Jews they knew that a person is not justified by works of the Law (e.g. circumcision), but by faith in Christ. And in the synopsis, we have of Peter's speech to the Jerusalem Council he makes it clear that "it is through the grace of our Lord Jesus Christ that we are saved" and he added "just as they [the Gentiles] are" (Acts 15:11). And he asked the question why … i.e. what is the purpose of "putting on the necks of these [Gentile] disciples a yoke [i.e. the keeping of the Law of Moses] that neither we [Jews] nor our fathers have been able to bear[5]?"

With such an argument, and recounting how Cornelius had been saved and had received the Holy Spirit, even though he had not been circumcised (nor baptised[6]), Peter argued against the view that the Gentiles had to be circumcised to be saved and had to keep the Mosaic Law. He may have let the side down in Syrian Antioch, but he fully supported Paul's position in Jerusalem.

---

[5] For a discussion on Jewish Christians and the Law of Moses during the Acts Period, see Appendix 1.

[6] For more on baptism see *Baptism: Rite and Reality* by Charles Ozanne, and *Baptisms in the Scriptures* by Brian Sherring, both published by The Open Bible Trust

12. Barnabas and Paul

When Peter had finished the whole assembly fell silent and they listened to Barnabas and Paul, as they told the assembly about the miraculous signs and wonders God had done through them amongst the Gentiles (Acts 15:12). However, I am sure they said much more than what has been recorded by Luke. One wonders what arguments Paul would have put forward to counteract those of the Judaisers – such arguments as we mentioned above.

The letter to the Galatians, written at the end of Acts 14 or at the beginning of Acts 15, was the first document written to deal with this issue, but even after the Jerusalem Council, there was still a group of Judaisers which ignored its decision. We learn that it was a problem that plagued the church in Rome and, in writing to them, Paul argued against their views in a more cogent and coherent manner. He went right back to Abraham.

> What then shall we say that Abraham, our forefather according to the flesh, discovered in this matter? If, in fact, Abraham was justified by works, he had something to boast about—but not before God. What does Scripture say? "Abraham believed God, and it was credited to him as righteousness." … Is this blessedness only for the circumcised, or also for the uncircumcised? We have been saying that Abraham's faith was credited to him as righteousness. Under what circumstances was it credited? Was it after he was circumcised, or before? It was not after, but before! (Romans 4:1-3; 9-10)

That Abraham was saved before he was circumcised, and considered righteous, solely on the ground that he had faith and believed God, would have been a powerful argument against the

Judaisers. This foundational teaching had been ignored in some Jewish circles, especially amongst the Pharisees. Paul, in his pre-Christian days, believed that with respect to legalistic righteousness, he was faultless (Philippians 3:6). However, he was to learn that such righteousness was as dirty rags (rubbish) compared to the righteousness that comes from God, given freely to those who have faith in Christ (Philippians 3:8-9). Such arguments as these may well have been part of Paul's armoury against the view that the Gentiles had to be circumcised to be saved.

But what about the view that the Gentiles had to keep the Mosaic Law? Why did some think they had to do so? And what was the role of the Law? It seems that some of the Jews, including the Judaisers, thought that the promises of God were secured only by obeying the Law. This may have been true for some of the promises (see, for example, Deuteronomy 28:1-14) but not all, and not the major ones.

> It was not through the law that Abraham and his offspring received the promise that he would be heir of the world, but through the righteousness that comes by faith. For if those who depend on the law are heirs, faith means nothing and the promise is worthless, because the law brings wrath. And where there is no law there is no transgression.
>
> Therefore, the promise comes by faith, so that it may be by grace and may be guaranteed to all Abraham's offspring—not only to those who are of the law but also to those who have the faith of Abraham. He is the father of us all. As it is written: "I have made you a father of many nations." He is our father in the sight of God, in whom he believed—the God who gives life to the dead and calls into being things that were not. (Romans 4:13-17)

Now Abraham, to whom such important promises were given, lived four hundred or more years before the Law was given. Thus keeping the Law can have no part in securing such promises. To be heirs, to have eternal life, is secured solely by faith and it is by God's grace and so it can be guaranteed. Nothing can be guaranteed if it depends upon a person's full obedience to the Law.

And Paul finished this chapter of Romans with a powerful passage which would have supported his argument at the Jerusalem Council.

> Against all hope, Abraham in hope believed and so became the father of many nations, just as it had been said to him, "So shall your offspring be." Without weakening in his faith, he faced the fact that his body was as good as dead—since he was about a hundred years old—and that Sarah's womb was also dead. Yet he did not waver through unbelief regarding the promise of God, but was strengthened in his faith and gave glory to God, being fully persuaded that God had power to do what he had promised. This is why "it was credited to him as righteousness." The words "it was credited to him" were written not for him alone, but also for us, to whom God will credit righteousness—for us who believe in him who raised Jesus our Lord from the dead. He was delivered over to death for our sins and was raised to life for our justification. (Romans 4:18-25)

Faith – being fully persuaded that God had the power to do what He had promised. Because Abraham had such faith, "it was credited to him as righteousness". He, an old man, had to believe that his descendants would be as numerous as the stars in the sky. The people of the Acts Period (both Jews and Gentiles), as well as people today, do not have to believe that their descendants are to be as numerous as the stars in the sky to gain righteousness from

God. Paul wrote that God will credit righteousness to us if we believe in Jesus, that He was delivered over to death for our sins and was raised to life for our justification.

However, notice how Paul brought in the Gentiles, by referring to Abraham as "a father of many nations" (Romans 4:17, quoting from Genesis 17:5). Israel may have been the chosen people, but they were not the only people. They may have been the number one nation, but they were not the sole nation. As we read through the Old Testament we find many references to how the Gentiles were to be blessed (starting in Genesis 12:3) and Israel's role should have been as a kingdom of priests to the other nations of the world (Exodus 19:6), and will be one day.

13. The judgment of James

James, in his judgment, picks up on Peter's references to the Gentiles, and quotes from Amos 9:11-12 to support his view.

> When they finished, James spoke up: "Brothers," he said, "listen to me. Simon [Peter] has described to us how God first intervened to choose a people for his name from the Gentiles. The words of the prophets are in agreement with this, as it is written:
> "'After this I will return
>   and rebuild David's fallen tent.
>   Its ruins I will rebuild,
>   and I will restore it,
>   that the rest of mankind may seek the Lord,
>   even all the Gentiles who bear my name,
>   says the Lord, who does these things'—
>   things known from long ago."
> (Acts 15:13-18)

James first refers to the God-fearing Gentile Cornelius. God had given a vision to Peter (three times) and the Holy Spirit had spoken to Peter, instructing him to welcome those whom Cornelius had sent. (God had also given a vision to Cornelius to instruct him to send for Peter.) Then, to prove to the Judaisers that what Peter had done was correct and that the bringing in of Gentiles was in harmony with God's will at that time, James quoted from the prophecy of Amos – but there were other Scriptures that he could have used. For example:

> "I, the Lord, have called you [Israel] in righteousness; I will take hold of your hand. I will keep you and will make you to

be a covenant for the people and a light for the Gentiles."
(Isaiah 42:6: a passage Paul referred to in Acts 13:47)

"It is too small a thing for you to be my servant to restore the
tribes of Jacob and bring back those of Israel I have kept. I
will also make you a light for the Gentiles, that my salvation
may reach to the ends of the earth." (Isaiah 49:6)

However, James preferred that quotation from Amos which also
spoke about the rebuilding of David's tent and the restoration of
Israel. When this was to happen was the question the disciples
asked the Lord just before His ascension, but which He refused to
answer.

Then they gathered around him and asked him, "Lord, are
you at this time going to restore the kingdom to Israel?" He
said to them: "It is not for you to know the times or dates the
Father has set by his own authority." (Acts 1:6-7)

Clearly Amos saw Israel going to the Gentiles *after* the restoration
of Israel but in Acts we have Gentiles being brought in *before* the
restoration. For an explanation of this, see Appendix 2, but let us
return to the Jerusalem Council and what James had to say.

"It is my judgment, therefore, that we should not make it
difficult for the Gentiles who are turning to God. Instead we
should write to them, telling them to abstain from food
polluted by idols, from sexual immorality, from the meat of
strangled animals and from blood. (Acts 15:19-20)

The judgment of the Council was that they did not want to make
life difficult for the new Gentile Christians; i.e. they saw no reason
why the Gentile Christians should keep the Law of Moses, and so
this was another decision that went against the Pharisaic Judaisers.

However, there was a problem, and this was a problem for the Jewish Christians.

Under the Mosaic Law there were certain things a person could do which rendered them ceremonially unclean, which placed restrictions on the Jews such as not being able to enter the inner courts of the temple in Jerusalem and offer their sacrifices. However, it made no difference whether a person was a Jew or a Gentile; if they did those things they were unclean ... and if another person had contact with them, then they, too, became unclean. The uncircumcised Gentile Christians, even if they went up to the temple in Jerusalem, were not allowed into the inner courts, so it mattered little to them whether they were clean or unclean. However, for the Jews, both Christian and non-Christian, this was a crucial issue. If a Christian Jew wanted to witness to a non-Christian Jew it was essential that the Christian Jew be ceremonially clean. However, if he had had contact with a Gentile, albeit a Christian one, suspicion would arise in the minds of non-Christian Jews as to whether that Gentile was clean or unclean ... and so they would query whether this Christian Jew was clean or unclean.

The judgment given by James dealt with this issue. He wanted the Christian Gentiles to abstain from four common causes of ceremonial uncleanness. He instructed them to:

1) Abstain from food polluted by idols;
2) Abstain from sexual immorality;
3) Abstain from the meat of strangled animals (which would still contain the blood of the animal);
4) Abstain from blood (either drinking it or getting it on themselves or both).

This would ensure that those Christian Jews who had dealings with Christian Gentiles remained ceremonially clean. And this would mean that they could also have fellowship and witness to the non-Christian Jews.

14. To sum up

Thus the Jerusalem Council decided that the Gentiles did not have to be circumcised to be saved; they were saved by grace through faith – just as Abraham was and they were.

The Council also decided that the Gentiles did not have to suffer the yoke of the Mosaic Law but that they should, at that time, abstain from four common Gentile behaviours which would render them unclean, a condition which would make life awkward, if not impossible, for the Jewish Christians of that time.

This decision was recorded in a letter (Acts 15:22-29) which was sent, not only to the church in Syrian Antioch, but to all the churches in Syria and Cilicia. And one suspects that when Paul wanted to revisit the towns where he had preached on his first missionary journey (especially those in Galatia) that his intention was to take a copy of the letter from the Jerusalem Council (Acts 15:36).

15. The Jerusalem Council and the Judaisers

One suspects that many of the Judaisers abided by the edict of the Jerusalem Council. However, some five years or so later, when Paul wrote to the church at Rome, there was clearly some concern regarding the Gentiles and circumcision and the Mosaic Law – issues Paul dealt with in Romans 4 and which we have quoted and commented on above.

But many years after that, when Paul had been under house arrest in Rome for nearly two years, he wrote to the Philippians and described those who still insisted on circumcision as "dogs" and "mutilators of the flesh" (Philippians 3:2).

And even later, some two years or so after that, the circumcision group was still operating. When writing to Titus, Paul stated that:

> For there are many rebellious people, full of meaningless talk and deception, especially those of the circumcision group. They must be silenced, because they are disrupting whole households by teaching things they ought not to teach—and that for the sake of dishonest gain. (Titus 1:10-11)

Initially, during Acts, when the first Gentiles came on the scene, the Judaisers may have genuinely misunderstood the role of circumcision. But now, some fifteen or so years later, they had no excuse. Not only that, some of them were saying the Gentiles had to be circumcised to be saved, so that they could demand payment from the Gentiles Christians for performing the operation!

16. The Jerusalem Council and the Gentiles

Some Christians today wonder whether or not they have to adhere to all four rules laid down in Acts 15:20. If we understand the judgment of the Jerusalem Council correctly, we will appreciate that the four restrictions placed on the Gentiles were for the benefit of the Jews of that time. So what happened to those Jews?

We saw earlier, on Paul's first missionary journey, that many of the Jews in the synagogues where he spoke (and especially the Jewish leadership) disputed and disagreed with him, opposed him and persecuted him. The Jews in Israel had rejected Jesus in person and had opposed and persecuted the Apostles during the Acts Period, rejecting their teaching that Jesus was the Christ (Messiah) and Son of God. Most of the Jews of the dispersion reacted similarly to the same message given by Paul. This went on for thirty years or so and when the Jewish leadership in Rome could not agree amongst themselves, Paul uttered, for the last time, the words of the judgmental prophecy of Isaiah six.

> "'Go to this people and say,
> "You will be ever hearing but never understanding;
>   you will be ever seeing but never perceiving."
> For this people's heart has become calloused;
>   they hardly hear with their ears,
>   and they have closed their eyes.
> Otherwise they might see with their eyes,
>   hear with their ears,
>   understand with their hearts
> and turn, and I would heal them.'"
> (Acts 28:26-27, quoting from Isaiah 6:9-10)

And he followed this by stating:

> "Therefore I want you to know that God's salvation has been sent to the Gentiles, and they will listen." (Acts 28:28)

This passage marks a watershed for Israel as a nation before God. They had been the chosen nation, the number one nation, but not any longer. Someday in the future they will regain that status but at the end of Acts the nation lost it. However, individual Jews, like individual Gentiles, could still be saved by having faith in God and believing that Jesus died for their sins and rose for their justification.

After this pronouncement, Paul spent two years under house arrest and during that time wrote Ephesians, Philippians, Colossians and Philemon. It seems he was then released and wrote 1 Timothy and Titus before being rearrested and writing 2 Timothy. In these letters we find some new and very different instructions. For example: the Mosaic Law, with its commandments and regulations, was set aside for the Jewish Christians.

> For he himself is our peace, who has made the two groups one and has destroyed the barrier, the dividing wall of hostility, by setting aside in his flesh the law with its commands and regulations. (Ephesians 2:14-15)

> Having cancelled the written code, with its regulations. (Colossians 2:14)

This included the abolition of physical circumcision, performed by a priest, and replaced with a spiritual circumcision performed by Christ.

In him you were also circumcised, in the putting off [cutting off] of the sinful nature, not with a circumcision done by the hands of men but with a circumcision done by Christ. (Colossians 2:11; see also Philippians 3:2-3)

The Gentiles of the Acts Period were never told to keep the Sabbath or any of the other holy days which were part of the Mosaic Law. Now Jewish Christians were freed from keeping these also.

Therefore do not let anyone judge you by what you eat or drink, or with regard to a religious festival, a New Moon celebration or a Sabbath day. (Colossians 2:16)

And we can see from this last quotation that the Jewish Christians were also freed from the dietary restrictions of the Mosaic Law; but how did all this affect the four rules of the Jerusalem Council? Let us refresh our memories as to what these were.

1) Abstain from food polluted by idols;
2) Abstain from sexual immorality;
3) Abstain from the meat of strangled animals (which would still contain the blood of the animal);
4) Abstain from blood (either drinking it or getting it on themselves or both).

It would seem that numbers 1, 3 and 4 were swept away by the abolition of the commands and regulations of the Mosaic Law. However, as to the second we read:

But among you there must not be even a hint of sexual immorality, or of any kind of impurity, or of greed, because these are improper for God's holy people. (Ephesians 5:3)

Put to death, therefore, whatever belongs to your earthly nature: sexual immorality, impurity, lust, evil desires and greed, which is idolatry. (Colossians 3:5)

The edict against sexual sins continued because not only are sexual sins against the Mosaic Law, they are also sins against a person's own body.

Flee from sexual immorality. All other sins a person commits are outside the body, but whoever sins sexually, sins against his own body. (1 Corinthians 6:18)

And our bodies are temples of God in which he lives by His Holy Spirit (1 Corinthians 3:16; 6:19; Ephesians 2:21-22).

17. In conclusion

An understanding of the Jerusalem Council will give us a better appreciation of what God was doing during the period of time covered by the Acts of the Apostles. However, the reason for those edicts, since the Jews as a nation became blind and deaf at the end of Acts, is no longer there. We may eat the meat of strangled animals but few of us are likely to encounter an animal which has been sacrificed to idols and I doubt if many of us would want to drink blood, though a few people like to eat black pudding (or blood pudding as it is called in some places). However, should we get blood on us, for some reason or other, we need not worry about being ceremonially unclean.

The one edict which is still important is that of sexual immorality. Being ceremonially unclean from such acts may not be relevant to us today, but it is still, none-the-less, a sin against our own bodies which may bring sexually transmitted diseases and Aids, to say nothing of unwanted pregnancies. And also, as mentioned above, our bodies are temples of the Holy Spirit.

Appendix 1: Jewish Christians and the Law of Moses during the Acts Period

There is a view in some Christian circles that the Law of Moses was abolished by Christ 'at' the Cross. However, we have many examples in the Acts of the Apostles of people like Paul keeping the Mosaic Law. For example, consider the following:

The Sabbath

- On the Sabbath day they entered the synagogue. (Acts 13:14)
- On the Sabbath we went outside the city gate to the river, where we expected to find a place to pray. (Acts 16:13)
- As his custom was, Paul went into the synagogue, and on three Sabbath days reasoned with them from the Scriptures. (Acts 17:2)
- Every Sabbath he reasoned in the synagogue. (Acts 18:4)

The Feasts of Leviticus 23

- We sailed from Philippi after the feast of Unleavened Bread. (Acts 20:6)
- Paul was in a hurry to reach Jerusalem, if possible, by the day of Pentecost. (Acts 20:16)

The Nazirite Vow of Numbers 6:18

- Before he sailed, Paul had his hair cut off at Cenchrea because of a vow he had taken. (Acts 18:18)
- … do what we tell you. There are four men with us who have made a vow. Take these men, join in their purification rites and pay their expenses, so that they can have their heads shaved. Then everybody will know there is no truth in these reports about you, but that you yourself are living in obedience to the law. (Acts 21:23-24)

Circumcision

- So he [Paul] circumcised him [Timothy] because of the Jews. (Acts 16:3)

Ceremonially Clean

- I was ceremonially clean when they found me in the temple courts. (Acts 24:18)

The High Priest

- I did not realize that he was the high priest; for it is written [in the Law]: 'Do not speak evil about the ruler of your people.' (Acts 23:5; see Exodus 22:28)

As mentioned above, the view in some Christian circles is that the Law was abolished 'at' the cross. This is not quite correct. The fact is that we read nothing about the Law being abolished until after Paul had pronounced the prophecy of judgment upon Israel in Acts 28:26-27, where he was quoting from Isaiah 6:9-10. In the ensuing two years he wrote both Ephesians and Colossians and in those we read:

> For he himself is our peace, who has made the two groups one and has destroyed the barrier, the dividing wall of hostility, by abolishing in his flesh the law with its commands and regulations. His purpose was to create in himself one new man out of the two, thus making peace, and in one body to reconcile both of them to God through the cross, by which he put to death their hostility. (Ephesians 2:14-16)

> Having cancelled the written code, with its regulations, that was against us and that stood opposed to us; he took it away, nailing it to the cross. (Colossians 2:14)

So it isn't until the end of the Acts Period that we learn that the Law has been abolished, cancelled, taken away. Now it is true that the Law was fulfilled when Christ sacrificed Himself on the cross, and God could have taken away the Law any time after that but He did not immediately do so. Why not?

We tend to give much emphasis to the fact that during the Acts of the Apostles, Gentiles started to be saved. However, the greater witness of the Acts Period was still to the people of Israel. Peter went to one Gentile (Cornelius) but he witnessed to thousands of Jews. Paul, everywhere he went, spoke first to the Jewish synagogue. God's desire was for Israel to be saved so the Apostles, and other Christian Jews, had to be credible witnesses to their fellow-countrymen. If Christian Jews, like Peter and Paul and thousands of other unnamed ones, had given up the Law and stopped keeping the Sabbath and practising circumcision, and if they had started eating pork and the meat of strangled animals, then their witness to the rest of Israel would have been seriously impaired. Those Jews who had not yet believed in Jesus would have discounted anything the Christian Jews said, as they would have been looked upon as unclean and called 'Gentile dogs'.

Thus it was essential during the time covered by the Acts of the Apostles that the Christian Jews continued in their observance of the Law of Moses. But, as stated in the text, the Jews in Israel had rejected Jesus in person and had opposed and persecuted the Apostles during the Acts Period, rejecting their teaching that Jesus was the Christ (Messiah) and Son of God. And most of the Jews of the dispersion reacted similarly to the same message given by Paul. This went on for thirty years or so until the end of Acts when, due to the blindness and deafness of Israel as a nation, God's salvation was sent to the Gentiles quite independently of Israel. It was at that time the Law was set aside. Individual Jews, like individual Gentiles, could still be saved by having faith in God and believing that Jesus died for their sins and rose for their justification. However, those new Christian Jews, after Acts, were no longer required to keep the Law.

Appendix 2: Gentiles brought in before the Restoration of the Kingdom to Israel

Although the Old Testament, and much of the New, is dominated by the people of Israel, the Gentiles always had a place, right from the time God spoke to Abraham.

> The LORD had said to Abram, "Go from your country, your people and your father's household to the land I will show you.
> "I will make you into a great nation,
>   and I will bless you;
> I will make your name great,
>   and you will be a blessing.
> I will bless those who bless you,
>   and whoever curses you I will curse;
> and all peoples on earth
>   will be blessed through you."
> (Genesis 12:1-3)

This was to be achieved by Israel becoming a holy nation and a kingdom of priests to the other nations of the world (Exodus 19:5-6), and bringing light to the Gentiles.

> "I, the Lord, have called you [Israel] in righteousness; I will take hold of your hand. I will keep you and will make you to be a covenant for the people and a light for the Gentiles." (Isaiah 42:6)

> "It is too small a thing for you to be my servant to restore the tribes of Jacob and bring back those of Israel I have kept. I

will also make you a light for the Gentiles, that you may bring my salvation to the ends of the earth." (Isaiah 49:6)

This continues into the New Testament, as Simeon stated when he picked up the child Jesus and said:

> "Sovereign Lord, as you have promised,
>> you may now dismiss your servant in peace.
> For my eyes have seen your salvation,
>> which you have prepared in the sight of all people:
> a light for revelation to the Gentiles,
>> and for glory to your people Israel."
> (Luke 2:29-32)

That being the case, why did the Lord send out the Twelve with specific instructions not to go into the way of the Gentiles and why did He say He was sent only to the lost sheep of the house of Israel? (See Matthew 10:5 and 15:24). The answer is:

> For I tell you that Christ has become a servant (minister, *KJV*) of the Jews on behalf of God's truth, to confirm the promises made to the patriarchs. (Romans 15:8)

Our Lord's ministry was to prepare Israel as a kingdom of priests, but that generation of Jews in Israel rejected Him. However, on the cross He prayed "Father, forgive them, for they do not know what they are doing" (Luke 23:34). That prayer was answered and during the Acts Period the Jews were given another opportunity. At first, things seemed to be going very well with 3,000 saved in Acts 2:41, a number which rose to 5,000 men (Acts 4:4) and many more men and women were added to this number (Acts 5:14).

None-the-less there were undertones of opposition from the Jewish leaders (Acts 4:1-21; 5:17-42) which came to a head with the persecution being so great that all Jewish Christians, except the Apostles, fled Jerusalem (Acts 8:1). So the goal of restoring Israel, and them becoming a kingdom of priests and being a witness to the Gentiles and a blessing to other nations, seemed to be slipping away. So was God going to close the door on Israel?

The man who wreaked havoc upon the church, one Saul of Tarsus, became a Christian and an Apostle. His commission was a two-fold one, as God told Ananias in Acts 9:15:

> This man is my chosen instrument to proclaim my name
> - to the Gentiles and their kings and
> - to the people of Israel.

However, the purpose in going to the Gentiles at that time was somewhat different from what many people imagine. It was not in the fulfilment of those Old Testament prophecies. In his letter to the Romans Paul gave the reason. He stated that at that time, i.e. during the latter part of the Acts Period, Israel had not fallen but had stumbled. .

> Again I ask: Did they stumble so as to fall beyond recovery? Not at all! Rather, because of their transgression, salvation has come to the Gentiles to make Israel envious … I am talking to you Gentiles. Inasmuch as I am the apostle to the Gentiles, I take pride in my ministry in the hope that I may somehow arouse my own people to envy and save some of them. (Romans 11:11,13-14)

Israel had stumbled and the Gentiles were to give them a helping hand to recover. How was this to be achieved? We read that the salvation of Gentiles during the Acts Period was to provoke Israel to envy, with the aim of stimulating them to believe in Christ and so be saved.

'Envy' is a funny thing. We can become envious of what a person does or has and envy can embitter us towards them. However, 'envy' can have a different effect: it can motivate us to want to be like that person, to emulate them. And this is the meaning in Romans 11:11-14, and which the *KJV* makes clear:

> If by any means I may provoke to emulation them which are my flesh, and might save some of them.

Paul goes on to explain this with the figure of an olive tree (Romans 11:17-21). Here Israel, as in many places, is likened to an olive tree, but this is an olive tree which is not bearing fruit. In an attempt to stimulate this tree into productivity some of the natural branches (some unbelieving Jews) were broken off and some branches from a wild olive tree (some believing Gentiles) were grafted in. Would the vigour and vitality of the wild olive stimulate the cultivated olive tree into bearing fruit?

Would Israel, witnessing God's grace being extended to Gentiles and them receiving the Holy Spirit, arouse the unbelieving Jews and cause them to emulate the Christian Gentiles and believe in Jesus?

This, wrote Paul, was the purpose of Gentile salvation during the Acts Period but it is not the purpose of Gentile salvation today, and it would be wrong to take this passage out of its historical context and apply it to today. But from the historical point of view, did it work? The answer is … it did not. As mentioned above, envy can provoke people to emulation, but it can have the opposite effect and this is exactly what happened in Pisidian Antioch where we read:

When the Jews saw the crowds, they were filled with jealousy and talked abusively against what Paul was saying. (Acts 13:45)

And what happened there seems to have been common practice. By the time we get to the end of Acts we read that Israel had hardened its heart which had become calloused. As a result, they had closed their ears to the argument from the Law and the Prophets and had closed their eyes to the evidence of the miracles (Acts 28:26-27). And as a result of this, judgment fell upon Israel and God's salvation was sent to the Gentiles (verse 28) … and the age of grace in which we live began.

Oh, the depth of
the riches of the wisdom and knowledge of God!
How unsearchable his judgments,
and his paths beyond tracing out!
(Romans 11:33)

About the author

Michael Penny was born in Ebbw Vale, Wales in 1943. He read Mathematics at the University of Reading before teaching for twelve years and becoming the Director of Mathematics and Business Studies at Queen Mary's College Basingstoke in Hampshire, England. In 1978 he entered Christian publishing, and in 1984 became the administrator of the Open Bible Trust, a position he held for seven years, before moving to the USA and becoming pastor of Grace Church in New Berlin, Wisconsin. He returned to Britain in 1999 and at present he is the editor and administrator of the Open Bible Trust and has written many books and numerous study booklets.

He has been the chair of Churches Together in Reading for ten years and in 2019 was elected chair of Churches Together in Berkshire. He has also been on the Advisory Committee to Reading University Christian Union for nine years. He is head chaplain at Reading College and is lead chaplain for Activate Learning Colleges including the City of Oxford College, Banbury College, Blackbird Leys College and Bracknell and Wokingham College.

He has appeared on Premier Radio and BBC Radio Berks on many occasions. He has an itinerant ministry which takes him into churches of different denominations, mainly in Berkshire and South Oxfordshire.

In 2019 the Bishop of Reading nominated him to receive the Maundy Money from the Queen for his services to Christianity, the Church and the Community, and he was one of the 93 men selected by Buckingham Palace from across the United Kingdom, along with 93 women.

More on Paul

Paul: A Missionary of Genius
By Michael Penny

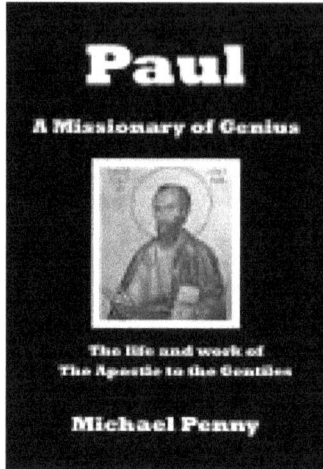

"One good reason why Christianity was triumphant was that it found in Saul of Tarsus, later St. Paul, a missionary of genius … Though himself a Jew, Paul took this new and startling religion out of Judaism into the world of the Gentiles"

So wrote the novelist J B Priestley.

But what do we know about this man Saul, who became Paul? This book deals with the life and work of the only person the New Testament calls "The Apostle to the Gentiles."

As well as covering all his life (from Tarsus, to Jerusalem, to Antioch and eventually on to Rome), this book also covers all his teaching from his two-fold commission in Acts (to go to the

Gentiles as well as Jews) to his final commission relating to the Body of Christ, where there is neither Jew nor Gentile.

This book will give Christians not only a better understanding of Paul and his writing, but also a better appreciation of the whole New Testament.

Fur further details please visit **www.obt.org.uk**
and the book can be ordered from that website.
It is also available as an e Book from Amazon and Apple
and as a paperback from Amazon.

Also by Michael Penny

Michael Penny has written on four of the major apostles

Paul: A Missionary of Genius
James: His life and letter
Peter: His life and letters
John: His life, death and writings

Some of his other the major works include

40 Problem Passages
Approaching the Bible
The Bible: myth or message?
Galatians: Interpretation and Application
Joel's Prophecy: Past and Present
The Miracles of the Apostles
Comments and Queries about Christianity
Comments and Queries about the New Testament
Following Philippians (with William Henry)
Introducing God's Plan (with Sylvia Penny)

He has also written many Bible Study Booklets,
as well as a number of study guides including:

Moving through Mark
Learning from Luke
The Manual on the Gospel of John
Going through Galatians
Exploring Ephesians
A Study Guide to Psalm 119
The Purpose of Parables
The Balanced Christian Life (Ephesians)
Search the Acts of the Apostles (with Neville Stephens)

For details of the above, please visit **www.obt.org.uk**

Free Magazine

Michael Penny is editor of *Search* magazine.

Publications of The Open Bible Trust must be in accordance with its evangelical, fundamental and dispensational basis. However, beyond this minimum, writers are free to express whatever beliefs they may have as their own understanding, provided that the aim in so doing is to further the object of The Open Bible Trust. A copy of the doctrinal basis is available on www.obt.org.uk or from:

THE OPEN BIBLE TRUST
Fordland Mount, Upper Basildon,
Reading, RG8 8LU, UK.

www.ingramcontent.com/pod-product-compliance
Lightning Source LLC
Chambersburg PA
CBHW060719030426
42337CB00017B/2922